I0795559

SNOWBOARDING

BY RACHEL GRACK

EPIC, AN IMPRINT OF BELLWETHER MEDIA BY FLUTTERBEE

EPIC BOOKS are no ordinary books. They burst with intense action, high-speed heroics, and shadows of the unknown. Are you ready for an Epic adventure?

This edition first published in 2027 by Bellwether Media, Inc.

Text copyright © 2027 by Bellwether Media, Inc. All rights reserved. No part of this publication may be reproduced, stored in any retrieval system, or transmitted in any form or by any means, electronic, mechanical, photocopying, recording, or otherwise, without written permission of the publisher.

EPIC and associated logos are trademarks and/or registered trademarks of Bellwether Media, Inc. Bellwether Media is a division of FlutterBee Education Group.

For information regarding permission, write to Bellwether Media, Inc., Attention: Permissions Department, 3500 American Blvd W, Suite 150, Bloomington, MN 55431.

Library of Congress Cataloging-in-Publication Data is available at www.loc.gov or upon request from the publisher.

ISBN: 9798898801007 (hardcover)
ISBN: 9798898802240 (ebook)

Editor: Kieran Downs   Designer: Jeffrey Kollock

Printed in the United States of America, North Mankato, MN.

TABLE OF CONTENTS

SHRED THE SNOW

A snowboarder rides down a mountain. They jump onto a rail.

They **grind** the rail until the end. They drop onto the fresh snow and keep speeding down the mountain!

LONGEST GRIND

The record for the longest rail grind in snowboarding is 275.5 feet (84 meters).

WHAT IS SNOWBOARDING?

Snowboarding is a popular winter sport. Riders slide down a snowy slope while standing on a board.

People snowboard on hillsides and mountains. Ski areas offer runs for every skill level.

FAMOUS LOCATION

MAMMOTH MOUNTAIN

LOCATION	Mammoth Lakes, California, United States
FAMOUS FOR	Long winters, a lot of snowfall, and 180 different runs

Snowboarders wear special boots. The boots attach to **bindings** on the board. Snowboards, boots, and bindings come in many different styles.

SNOWBOARDING GEAR

Riders wear snow jackets and pants. Gloves should be warm and waterproof. Helmets and goggles keep riders safe.

THE HISTORY OF SNOWBOARDING

Sherman Poppen invented the Snurfer in 1965. It was a board for surfing on the snow. Riders steered with a rope.

In 1972, Dimitrije Milovich came up with a new **design**. He created Winterstick. It was the first snowboard company.

Jake Burton Carpenter started Burton Boards in 1977. His boards had bindings and fins for better control.

Later styles looked more like a skateboard. This shape was better for tricks.

STILL BOARDING

Burton snowboards are still popular today.

JAKE BURTON CARPENTER

BURTON SNOWBOARD

FAMOUS FACE

CHLOE KIM

BIRTHDAY	April 23, 2000
HOMETOWN	Torrance, California
FAMOUS FOR	Two-time Olympic gold medal winner in halfpipe and the youngest woman to win gold in halfpipe

TIMELINE

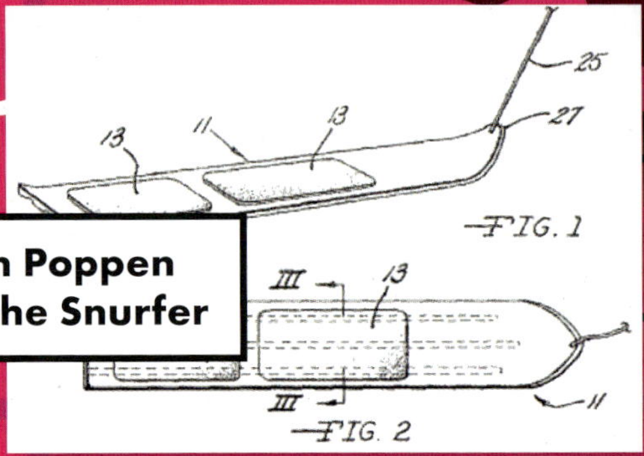

1965 Sherman Poppen invents the Snurfer

1972 Winterstick becomes the first snowboarding company

1977 Jake Burton Carpenter creates Burton Boards

1997 Snowboarding is a part of the first Winter X Games

1998 Snowboarding is added to the Winter Olympics

Snowboarding was part of the first **Winter X Games** in 1997.

Snowboarding was added to the **Winter Olympics** in 1998. Riders raced in **giant slalom**. They showed off tricks on the **halfpipe**.

1997 WINTER X GAMES

PARALLEL GIANT SLALOM, WINTER OLYMPICS

SNOWBOARDING TODAY

Snowboarding has many **disciplines**. Riders perform tricks in halfpipe events.

slopestyle

HIGHEST AIR

Valentino Guseli holds the world record for highest air on a snowboard. He jumped 37.7 feet (11.5 meters).

Slopestyle includes jumps and grinds on rails. Riders do sky-high flips and other tricks in **big air**. Judges rate their skills and style.

Riders race one another in snowboard cross. They speed over jumps and tight turns. The fastest racer wins!

parallel slalom

snowboard cross

Snowboarders race through side-by-side courses in **parallel slalom**. The fastest runs reach the next round.

HOW TO

OLLIE

Top riders **compete** in events. The Winter X Games and the Winter Olympics feature the best riders in the world.

Movies such as *The Art of Flight* show off popular riders doing daring tricks. Feel the thrill!

GLOSSARY

big air—a freestyle event where riders perform high jumps, spins, and flips

bindings—straps that hold a rider's boots to a snowboard

compete—to try to win something that someone else is also trying to win

design—a plan for a building, object, or pattern

disciplines—types of contests

giant slalom—a snowboard race through gates that is on a long, steep course

grind—to ride a snowboard down a rail

halfpipe—an event where riders do tricks on a U-shaped, high-sided ramp used in snowboarding, skateboarding, and skiing

parallel slalom—a race in which two riders compete head-to-head through side-by-side courses

slopestyle—a freestyle snowboarding event that takes place on a course with rails, boxes, and jumps

Winter Olympics—a worldwide winter sports contest held in a different country every four years

Winter X Games—a yearly extreme sports event that includes snowboarding and skiing

TO LEARN MORE

AT THE LIBRARY

Conaghan, Bernard. *Snowboarding.* New York, N.Y.: Crabtree Publishing, 2023.

Grack, Rachel. *Kitesurfing.* Minneapolis, Minn.: Bellwether Media, 2027.

Schuh, Mari. *Snowboarding.* Mankato, Minn.: Amicus Ink, 2020.

ON THE WEB

FACTSURFER

Factsurfer.com gives you a safe, fun way to find more information.

1. Go to www.factsurfer.com.
2. Enter "snowboarding" into the search box and click 🔍.
3. Select your book cover to see a list of related content.

INDEX

The images in this book are reproduced through the courtesy of: martinscphoto, front cover, p. 1; cppzone, front cover, pp. 1, 4; Vasily Merkushevm front cover, p. 1; Dmytro Vietrov, p. 2; vitaliy_melnik, p. 3; helivideo, p. 5; Kirill Grekov, p. 6; Image Professionals GmbH/ Alamy Stock Photo, p. 7 (left); Chizhevskaya Ekaterina, p. 7 (right); rtranq, p. 8; Nomad_Soul, p. 8 (inset); yanlev, p. 8 (snowboard); Ocskay Mark, p. 8 (bindings); Alex Photo, p. 8 (boots); anatoliy_gleb, p. 9; Dmitry Molchanov, p. 9 (jacket); luckybusiness, p. 9 (helmet); Sergey Mironov, p. 9 (goggles); Nix EP/ Wikimedia Commons, p. 10 (snurfer); adsR/ Alamy Stock Photo, p. 10; aleksey ipatov, p. 11; Studio MDF, p. 12 (inset); Johannes Kroemer/ Getty Images, pp. 12, 14 (1977); David Ramos/ Getty Images, p. 13 (left); Adam Pretty/ Getty Images, p. 13 (right); Xinhua/ Alamy Stock Photo, p. 13 (bottom); Sherman R. Poppen/ Wikimedia Commons, p. 14 (1965); Harry How/ Getty Images, p. 14 (1997); Shaun Botterill/ Getty Images, p. 14 (1998); NurPhoto/ Getty Images, p. 15; JOAN C FAHRENTHOLD/ AP Images, p. 15 (inset); Kofimage, p. 16; Cameron Spencer/ Getty Images, p. 17; mountainpix, p. 18 (inset); KIRILL KUDRYAVTSEV/ Getty Images, p. 18; Millo Moravski/ Agence Zoom/ Getty Images, p. 20 (inset); Matthias Hangst/ Getty Images, p. 20; Mark Agnor, p. 21; The Art of Flight/ Wikimedia Commons, p. 21 (inset).